Swordplay:

an anonymous illustrated Dutch treatise for fencing with rapier, sword and polearms from 1595

Transcription, English translation and interpretation by Reinier van Noort

Freelance Academy Press, Inc.
www.FreelanceAcademyPress.com

Freelance Academy Press, Inc., Wheaton, IL 60189
www.freelanceacademypress.com

Printed in the United States of America
by Publishers' Graphics

19 18 17 16 15 14 13 12 11 10 1 2 3 4 5

ISBN 978-1-937439-26-2

Library of Congress Control Number: 2015954362

To Matt Galas, for his helpful comments on the initial transcription and translation, and for encouraging a more thorough interpretation and discussion, without which this project might never have happened.

About the Author

Reinier van Noort started training in Historical European Martial Arts in 2005, when he first took up longsword fencing. About five years later, Reinier encountered the rapier through translating Johannes Georgius Bruchius' Scherm-ofte Wapen-konste, and a new passion was found. Since then, Reinier has been actively working on researching, learning and teaching rapier fencing and related martial arts, with a focus on the Netherlands in the 17th century. He founded the School voor Historische Schermkunsten (School for Historical Fencing Arts), the first HEMA school in the Netherlands to focus on rapier fencing, and has taught workshops at events and seminars throughout Europe. Currently, Reinier teaches Rapier fencing in Oslo (Norway) with the Frie Duellister. In addition, he has produced and published a number of English translations of treatises written in Dutch, German and French. His projects include: Lessons on the Thrust, an English translation of Jéann Daniel L'Ange's Deutliche und gründliche Erklärung der Adelichen und Ritterlichen freyen Fecht-Kunst (1664); and Of the Single Rapier, an English translation of Johannes Georgius Bruchius Grondige Beschryvinge van de Edele ende Ridderlijcke Scherm- ofte Wapen-konste (1671).

For his work, Reinier received a Best Researcher Award at the 2014 HEMA Scholar Awards.

Contents

Introduction

The anonymous manuscript MS U 423.792 in the Newberry library in Chicago, dated 1595, is one of the oldest known martial arts treatises from the Low Countries. It treats fencing with the single sword, rapier and dagger, dussack and shield, rapier and buckler, halberd, and full pike, in both illustrations and text, and provides an interesting early perspective on the otherwise poorly documented Dutch martial tradition.

Currently, only a small number of martial arts treatises from the Netherlands is known to exist (see also Galas and Steenput, 2011). One of the oldest of these treatises is anonymous manuscript MS folio U 423.792. This manuscript is held in the Newberry Library in Chicago, which purchased it in 1957 from F. & G. Staack in Camden, Maine, for $256.50. The 22x28cm manuscript consists of 17 folios, containing 3 pages with text only, 26 pages with coloured illustrations of fighting techniques with various weapons, and 2 pages with both illustration and text. The final illustrated page contains part of an illustration which appears to have carried over to the next page, suggesting the manuscript is incomplete. The manuscript is written in Dutch, and is dated 1595 on one of its pages.

The 1595 date places MS folio U 423.792 in an interesting period in the history of the Netherlands, when rebellion against Philip II of Spain had effectively led to independence of the Calvinist Northern provinces from Catholic Spain. With the Spanish forces occupied fighting France, Maurice of Orange succeeded in conquering important cities outside the heartland of Holland, thus expanding the holdings of the United Provinces. It was also in 1595 that Cornelis de Houtman set sail on the first Dutch spice trade expedition, and his was soon followed by more such expeditions, with Olivier van Noort being the first Dutchman to circumnavigate the globe from 1598-1601. The results of these and similar expeditions led to the formation of the Dutch East India Company (VOC – Vereenigde Oost-Indische Compagnie) in 1602. These developments in turn led to a Golden Age in Dutch history that would roughly span the 17th century, reaching its peak just before the disaster year 1672, when the Dutch Republic was attacked by armies from Münster and Cologne, England, and France.

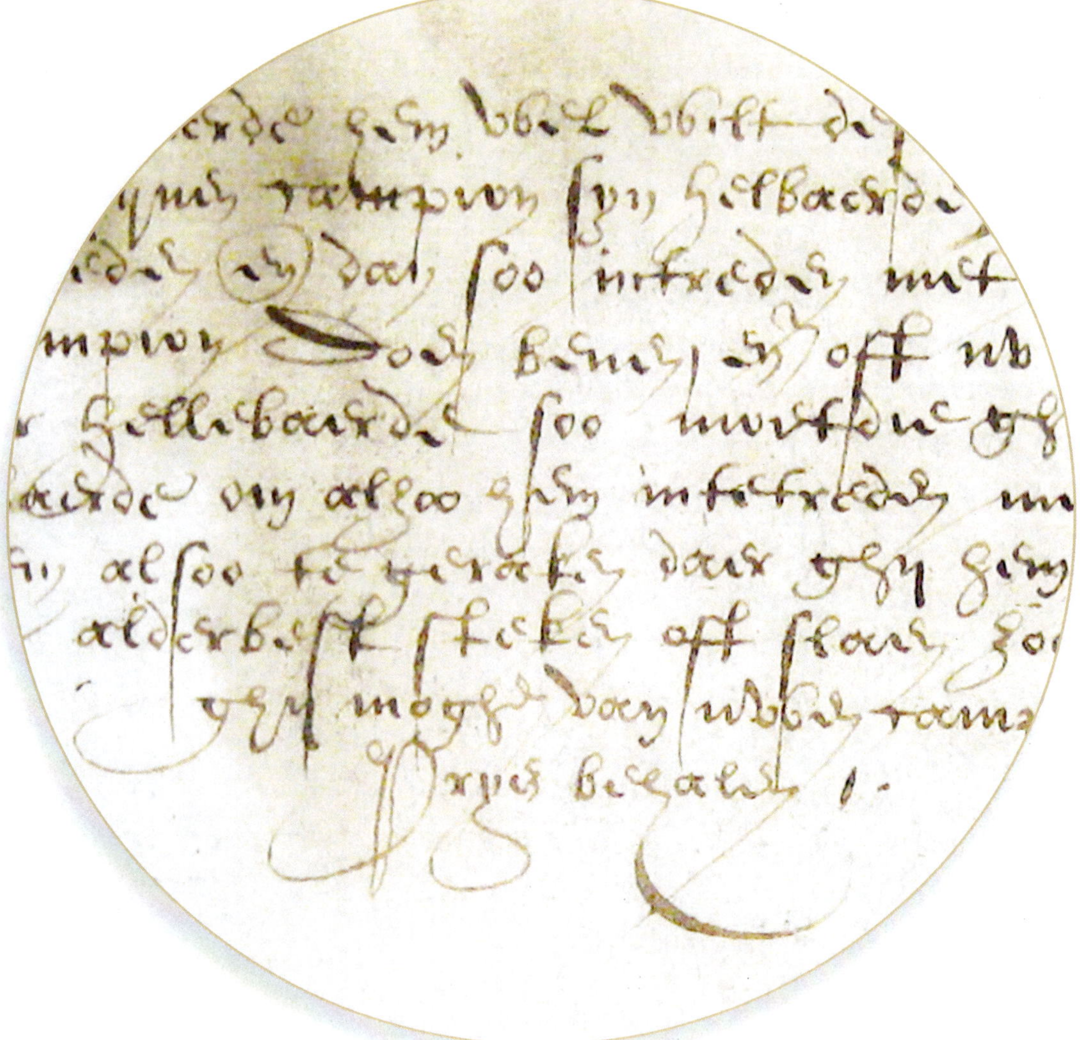

Transcription, Translation and Illustrations

Five of the 34 preserved pages of MS folio U 423.792 contain hand-written text. This text details fighting with a selection of weapons, including rapier and dagger (*Rappier en poinniaerten*), dussack and shield "after the Turkish manner" (*Tashack near teurckschen wysen*), rapier and buckler (Rappier en bouckelet), halberd (*helbaede*) and pike (*Spice*). The text is written in a cursive script, which in places is difficult to read. Smudges further make the writing nearly illegible in places. In the following transcription, text that was difficult to decipher has been placed between brackets ('<' and '>'), and brackets combined with an ellipsis ('<...>') are used to indicate where one or more words are completely illegible. The same indications are carried over into the English translation. Furthermore, words added to the English translation for clarity have been placed between square brackets.

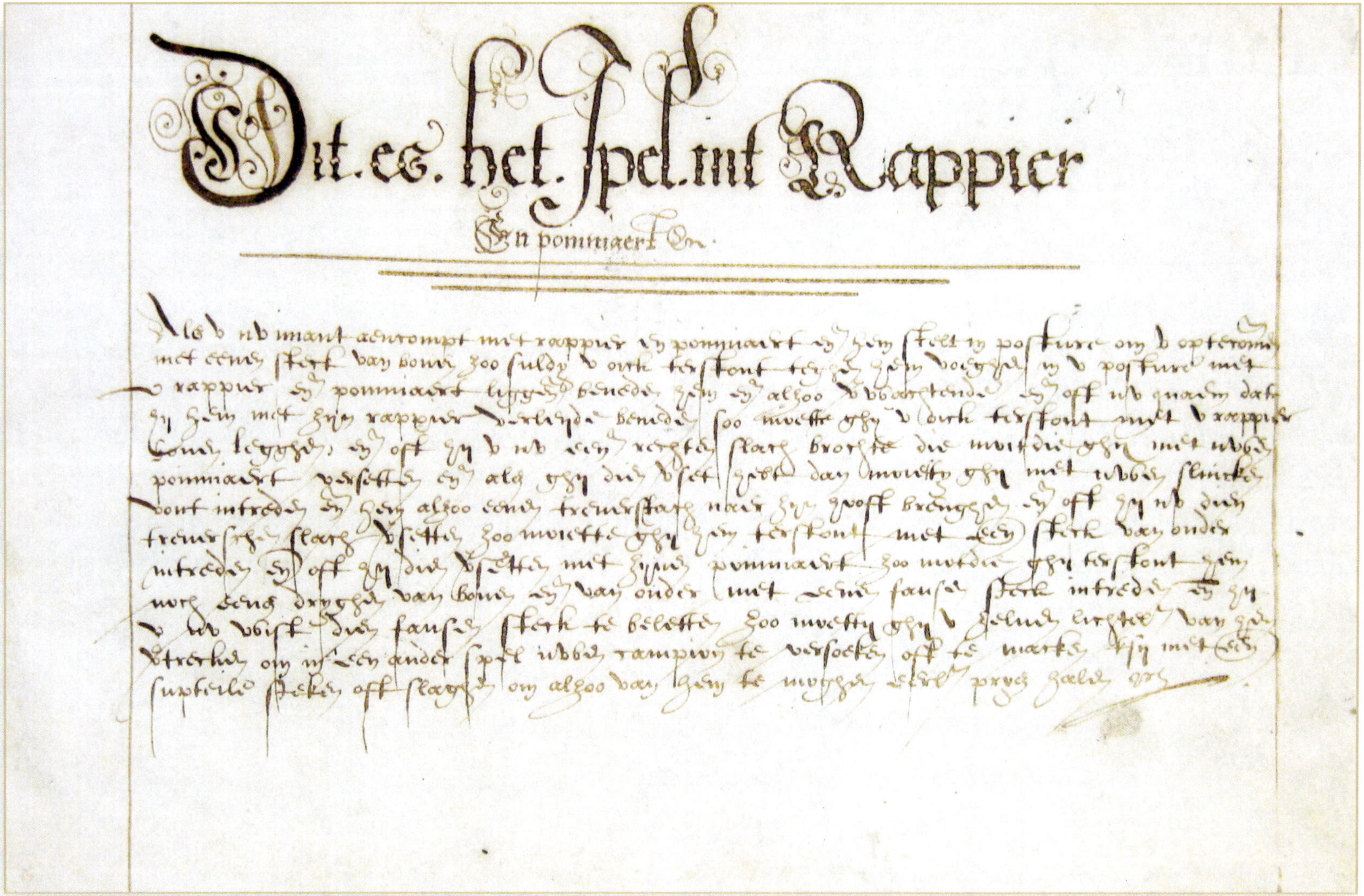
Dit es het spel met Rappier

En pommaert

Folio 1r

Transcription:

Dit es het Spel int Rappier

En poinniaerten.

Als u nu imant aencompt[1] *met rappier en poinniaert en hem stelt in posture om u optecommen met eenen steck van boven zoo suldy u oick terstont teghen hem voeghen in u posture met u rappier ende poinniaert liggende beneden hem ende alzoo verwachtende ende oft nu quaem dat hy hem met zyn rappier verleyde beneden soo moette ghy u oick terstont met u rappier boven legghen, ende oft hy u nu eenen rechten slach brochte die moitdie ghy met uwen poinniaert versetten ende als ghy dien verset hebt dan moietty ghy met uwen slincken vout intreden ende hem alzoo eenen treverstach*[2] *naer zyn huoft brenghen ende oft hy nu dien*

---

1 Alternatively, this might read "aencampt", changing the meaning of this first sentence to "If you get into a fight with someone [armed] with rapier and dagger, ...".

2 The author likely meant "treverslach"

treverschen slach versetten zoo moiette ghy hem terstont met eenen steck van onder intreden ende oft hy dien versetten met zynen poinniaert zoo motdie ghy terstont hem noch eens dryghen van boven ende van onder met eenen fausen steck intreden en hy u nu wist dien fausen steck te beletten zoo moetty ghy u zelven lichtelijk van hem vertrecken om in een ander spel[3] *uwen campion te versoeken oft te macken tsy met eenen supteile steken oft slaghen om alzoo van hem te moghen eerlijk prys halen* <...>.

Translation:

This is the play with the rapier and dagger.

If someone comes at you with rapier and dagger, and he places himself in [a] posture to come at you with a thrust from above, then you should immediately also move into your posture with your rapier and dagger lying beneath him, and so wait. And if it happens that he shifts with his rapier below, then

3 As pointed out by Matt Galas, the words "spel" (play), "campion" (literally: champion, here: opponent), and "prys halen" (obtain [the] prize) are also commonly used in contemporary Belgian fencing guild documents. This may suggest a sportive context as these documents often deal with regulations for fencing competitions.

you must immediately also position yourself with your rapier above. And if he delivers a right[4] blow at you, you must parry it with your dagger, and when you have parried it, then you must step in with your left foot and so deliver him a traversing[5] blow to his head. And if he parries that traversing blow, then you must immediately step in at him with a thrust from below; and if he parries that with his dagger, then you must immediately again threaten him from above, and step in with a false[6] thrust from below. And if he manages to prevent that false thrust, then you must nimbly depart from him, to attempt to finish off your opponent in another play[7], either with subtle thrusts or blows, and to thus honourably obtain [the] prize[8] from him.

---

4 Possible translations for "rechten slach" are "straight blow" and "right blow". The latter was chosen here, as it parallels the use in contemporary English works.

5 In the French translation of Giganti (1619 – a bilingual French and German version), a *coupe de taille traverse* refers to a riverso, i.e. a diagonal downwards cut from the left. However, this might be a direct translation of the German version which distinguishes between a *Haw* made *strack* (straight) or *in die querre* (across), i.e. it distinguishes between a straight vertical blow and a blow that is either horizontal or at least diagonal (crossing the center line). The German version of Giganti most likely mis-translates the original Italian here. The "treverschen slach" could either mean a reverse blow (making the *rechten slach* a diagonal blow from the right), or a horizontal blow (making the *rechten slach* a straight vertical blow)."

6 The word "fausen" is likely the same word as the French "faux", meaning "false" or "fake".

7 As Suggested by Saskia Roselaar "oft te macken" in 16th century Dutch could mean "to get away". An alternative translation for this sentence would then be "...to implore your opponent in another play to get away...".

8 An alternative translation for "prys" could be "praise".

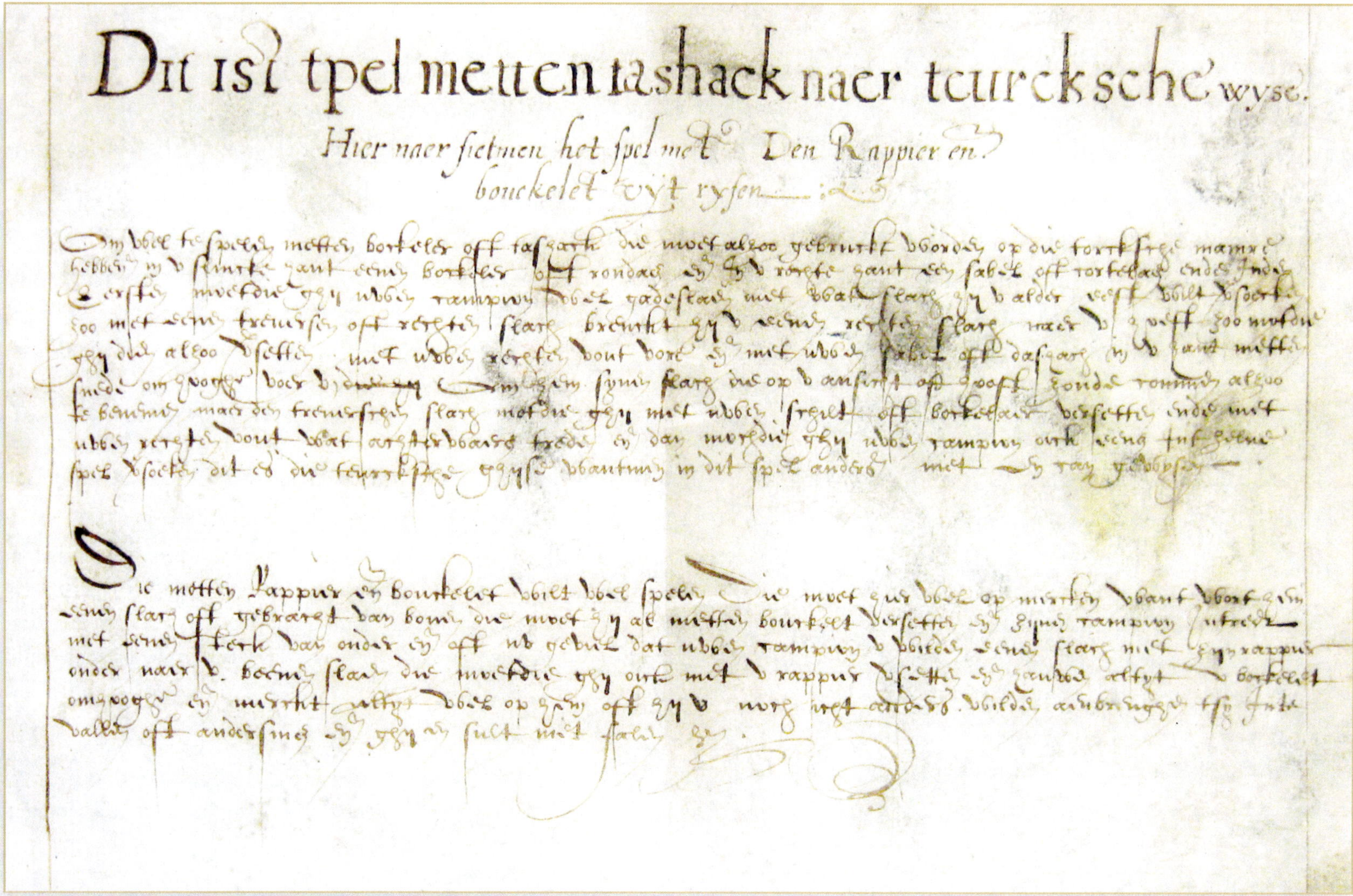

Dit ist spel metten tasback naer teurcksche wyse.

Hier naer sietmen het spel met Den Rappier en bouckelet vyt rysen

[illegible]

[illegible]

Folio 2r

Transcription:

Dit ist tpel metten tashack[9] naer teurckschen wysen.

Hier naer sietmen het spel met Den Rappier en bouckelet uijt rysen.

Om wel te spelen metten bockeler oft tashack die moet alzoo gebruckt worden op die torcksche manire hebbende in u slincke hant eenen bockeler oft rondas ende in u rechte hant een sabel oft cortelas ende Inden eersten moetdie ghy uwen campion wel gadeslaen met wat slach hy u alder eest wilt versoecken zoo met eenen treversen oft rechten slach brenckt hy u eenen rechten slach naer u hoeft zoo motdie ghy dien alzoo versetten met uwen rechten vout vore ende met uwen sabel oft dashach in u hant metten snede om huoghe voer u, die hy om hem synen slach die op u ansicht oft hooft zoude commen alzoo te benemen maer den treverschen slach motdie ghy met uwen schilt of bockelaer versetten ende met uwen rechten vout wat achterwaers treden en dan mochdie ghy uwen campion oick eens Int selve

---

9 The word "Tashack", or dussack, generally refers to a short single-edged sword; the word appears to be of Eastern or Central European origin. In Germany in the 16th century the word dussack was adopted to mean a wooden or leather practice weapon for single-edged short swords.

spel versoeken dit es die teurcksche ghyse wantmen in dit spel anders niet sij can gewysen.

Die metten Rappier en bouckelet wilt wel spelen Die moet hier wel op mercken want wort hem eenen slach oft gebracht van boven die moet hy al metten bouckelt versetten en zijnen campion Intreden met eenen steck van onder ende oft nu geviel dat uwen campion u wilden eenen slach met zijn rappier onder naer u beenen slaen die moetdie ghy oick met u rappier versetten ende hauwen altyt u bockelet ombuoghe ende merckt altyt wel op hem oft hy u noch icht anders wilden aenbrenghen tsy <Int> vallen oft andersins ende ghy en sult niet falen.

Translation:

This is the play with the dussack after the Turkish manner.

Afterwards the play with the rapier and buckler is presented.

To play well with the targe[10] or dussack they must be used thus in the Turkish manner, having in your left hand a targe or rotella and in your right hand a sabre or cutlass. And first you must observe your opponent well, [to see] what blow he wants to try against you first, whether with a traversing or [a] right

10 Bockeler (c.f. the French word "bouclier") refers to a larger, round shield that is used strapped to the arm.

blow. If he delivers you a right blow to your head, then you must parry it thus, with your right foot forwards and with your sabre or dussack in your hand with the edge upwards in front of you to take his blow that would [otherwise] come at your face or head from him. But the traversing blow you must parry with your shield or buckler, and step backwards somewhat with your right foot; and then you may also try your opponent in the same play. This is the Turkish way, for one cannot use them differently in this play[11].

He who wants to play well with the rapier and buckler[12] must note this well; that if a blow is delivered to him from above, he must parry that with the buckler and step in at his opponent with a thrust from below. And if it should happen that your opponent wants to strike you a blow with his rapier below to your legs, you must also parry that with your rapier, and always hold your buckler up high and always mark him well, [to see] if he wants to deliver something else at you, either attacking, or otherwise, and you will not fail.

---

11 The meaning of the word "gewysen" in this sentence (which also rhymes in Dutch) is difficult to interpret. We have chosen "use", interpreting "sij" to refer to the weapons.

12 Bouckelet, i.e. a "small shield". A small hand-held shield known in English as a "buckler".

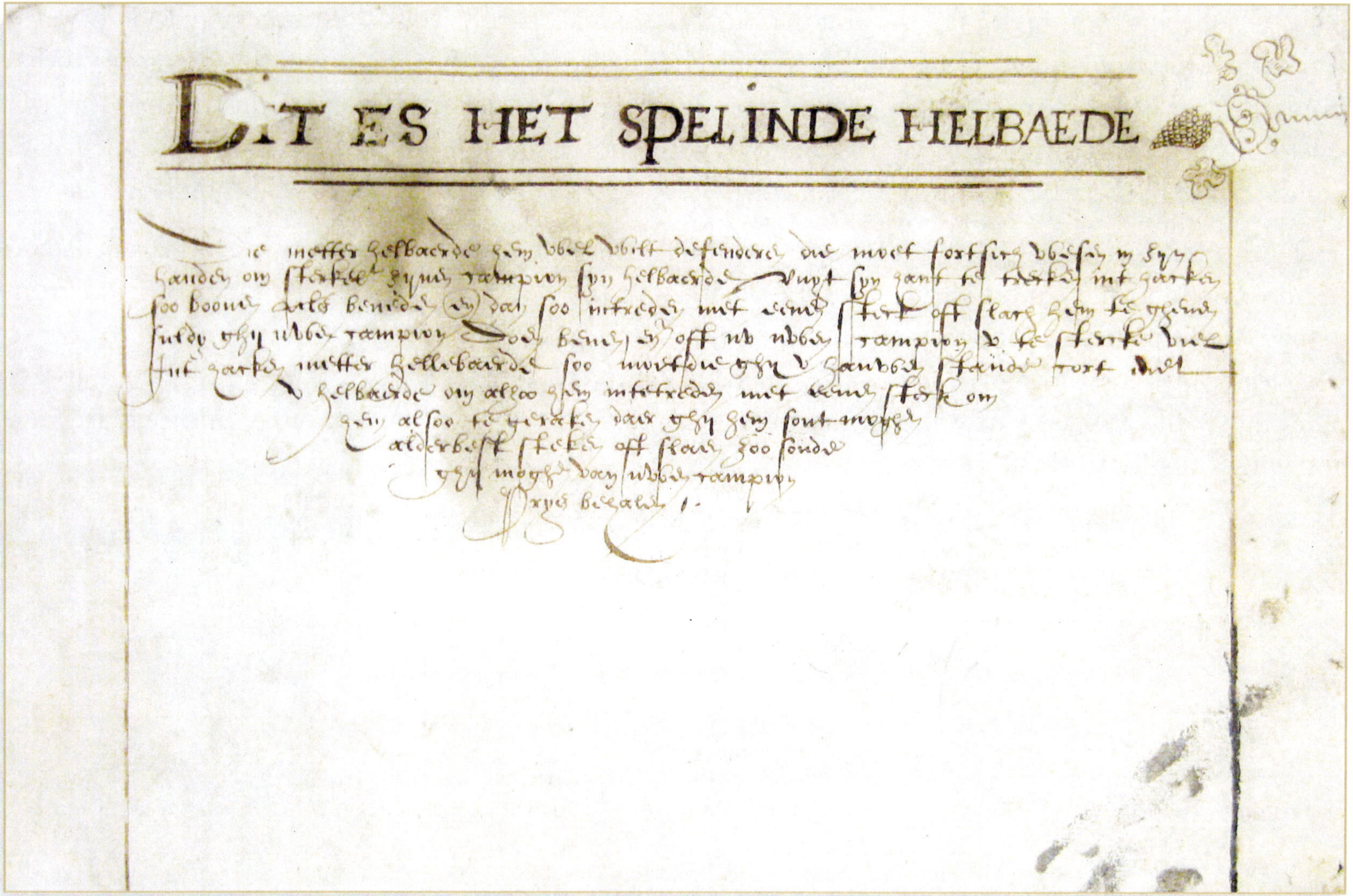

DIT ES HET SPEL INDE HELBAEDE

Die metter helbaerde hem wel wilt defenderen die moet fortsich wesen in syn
handen om sterkelic synen rampion syn helbaerde vuyt syn gans te trecken uut garken
soo boven als beneden en dan soo intreden met eenen stek oft slach hem te geven
sulde ghy uwen rampion doen beneden oft uut uwen rampion u te sterke wel
sut garden metter hellebaerde soo moetsdie ghy u handen staende voort met
u helbaerde en alsoo ghy intreden met eenen stek om
hem alsoo te geraken daer ghy hem sout mogen
alderbest steken oft slaen zoo sonde
ghy mogen van uwen rampion
Prys bezalt .

Folio 3r

Transcription:

Dit es het spel inde helbaede.

Die metter helbaerde hem wel wilt defenderen die moet fortsich wesen in zyn

handen om sterkelijk zynen campion syn helbaerde uyt syn hant te trecken int hacken

soo booven als beneden en dan soo intreden met eenen steck oft slach hem te gheven

suldy ghy uwen campion Doen beven ende oft nu uwen campion u te stercke viel

Int hacken metter hellebaerde soo moetdie ghy u hauwen stande cort <met>

u helbaerde om alzoo hem intetreden met eenen steck om

hem alsoo te geraken daer ghy hem sout moghen

alderbest steken oft slaen soo soude

ghy moghen van uwen campion

Prys behalen.

Translation:

This is the play with the halberd.

He who wants to defend himself well with the halberd must be strong in his hands to strongly pull the opponent's halberd out of his hand in hewing both above and below, and then step in while giving him a thrust or blow, [and thus] you will make your opponent shiver [with fear]. And if your opponent should be too strong for you in hewing with the halberd, then you must hold your stance short <with> your halberd, in order to step in at him with a thrust, to then hit him where you might best thrust or strike him. In this way you may obtain [the] prize from your opponent.

In addition to the above text, MS folio U 423.792 contains 28 pages with gouache drawings in colour, showing men fencing with various weapons. The fencers are dressed in clothing that is typical of the late sixteenth century, with spacious pantaloons, fastened just below the knee, stockings, doublets, (sleeveless) jerkins and ruffs. In a number of illustrations the fencers wear particularly elaborate and voluminous pantaloons drooping well below the knee at which they are tied. In particular, this is the case in the first three single sword plates (which show shorter, wider, round-tipped cutting blades, as opposed to the long, narrow, sharply-pointed blades shown in the remainder of the manuscript), the first three halberd plates, and the plates showing pike fencing, These spacious pantaloons are reminiscent of the dress worn by the "Landsknecht" mercenaries of the sixteenth century, which is interesting as the fighters wearing them all appear to be fighting with more military weapons, suggesting a differentiation between civilian and military fencing styles.

The first eight illustrations show fencing with single swords. The following two illustrations show an unarmed man defending himself against a man armed with a sword. Next, five plates show fencing with sword and dagger. This is followed by two plates showing men with curved swords and shields, three plates of sword and buckler fencing, five plates of halberd fighting, and one plate, spread over two pages, both containing text and showing men fighting with long pikes. The final page of the manuscript shows one half of another illustration of pike fighting.

In most illustrations, the fencers are shown standing in quite upright stances, with their feet roughly three feet apart. The front leg is usually bent, suggesting a somewhat forward weighted pose, though the torso is often leaning back. In many illustrations, the back foot is partly lifted off the ground, suggesting forward movement. The left hand, when not holding a weapon, is either placed at the hip or back, or is held out for defense or balance. Based on the available information, then, the fighting style shown thus has much in common with other mid- to late-16th century fencing styles such as those described by Italian authors like Manciolino (1531)and Marozzo (1536) (see also Leoni, 2010), and for instance de Sainct Didier (1573 – see also Hyatt and Wilson, 2009).

If we look at the manner in which the sword is gripped, we see that on some illustrations it is held in a relatively tight fist grip, allowing little rotation of the sword within the hand, while in other illustrations, a more loose "handshake grip" is used. Despite the use of complex-hilted swords, none of the fencers appears to finger the crossguard, as is common in for instance Marozzo (1536) but is not shown in de Sainct Didier (1573).

Considering the techniques shown in the various sections of illustrations in the manuscript; single sword fencing, sword and dagger fencing, sword and shield fencing (containing both dussack and shield and rapier and bucker), halberd fencing and pike fencing, we notice that the sword sections each start with one illustration showing the fencers drawing their swords and taking up guard positions. The drawing of the swords is then followed by a succession of illustrations showing binds and guards. In the single sword section, this is finished off with two illustrations showing an unarmed man defending himself against an assailant with a sword. In the illustrations showing fencing with sword and dagger, when taking guards a high sword is often opposed with a high dagger and a low sword, and vice versa, as is also shown in the single sword illustration on page 7r. Similar to the sword sections, the halberd section shows two binds, followed by a leg hook, a thrust against a fallen opponent, and a neck hook. The only remaining complete pike illustration likewise shows two fencers in guard positions.

Single Sword Fencing

The first eight illustrations show fencing with single swords. The first three of these illustrations show men fencing with swords that have relatively short and wide cutting blades with a rounded tip. These swords are rather similar to the katzbalger blades commonly associated with Landsknecht mercenaries, except that they have a straight cross and one or two knuckle bows. This may indicate a more military application of the techniques illustrated on these pages. Swords shown in the remainder of this section, and in rest of the manuscript, have significantly longer and narrower blades that end in a sharply pointed tip. All of these longer swords have straight crosses and side rings. Many of the swords in the single sword section also have a knuckle bow, while the swords in the sword and dagger and sword and buckler sections do not.

The fencing style shown in the single sword section (and other sections of the manuscript) is more comparable to the (earlier) sixteenth century cut-and-thrust ("Bolognese") style of, for instance, authors like Manciolino (1531), Marozzo (1536), de Sainct Didier (1575) and Viggiani (1575), than to the closest Dutch treatises; Bailly (1602-1608 – see also Galas and Steenput, 2011) and Thibault (1630 – see also Greer, 2006), who show later rapier fencing. Important differences with these later Dutch treatises are for instance the guards used by the fencers in this manuscript, in which the point is commonly out of presence, the amount of cutting in the single sword section, and the position of the left hand, also in the single sword section, which is held at the back out of reach of cuts, rather than forward in defence. Manuscript MS U 423.792 thus provides an interesting and important view on fencing in the Lowlands before typical rapier fencing styles were commonly adopted.

As in general, the order of the illustrations follows the order of the text chapters, the presence of the single sword fencing illustrations before the other illustrations suggests that text on single sword fencing may once have preceded the text on fencing with rapier and dagger. Unfortunately, these pages have not been preserved with what remains of the manuscript.

1. Two men preparing to fence (4r)

The man on the left stands upright, with his right hand on the sword grip, ready to draw his sword from its scabbard. The other stands with his legs apart, right foot forward, and has just drawn his sword from the scabbard. His left hand holds the scabbard behind his back and his right arm at is shoulder height, with his sword pointing somewhat backwards over his right shoulder.

2. A downward diagonal cut from the right (4v)

The man on the right appears to give a downward diagonal cut from the right, while standing with the right foot in front. This cut is parried in a hanging guard by the man on the left, who stands with his left foot in front. Both men stand with the back of their left hand placed against their hip. Alternatively, from the previous plate, the fencer on the left may have stepped back, cutting up into a parry. Note the bend in the wrist of the fencer on the right.

3. A low cut at the front leg (5r)

Here, a low cut at the right (front) leg is made by the man on the right. This cut is parried by the man on the left who, standing with the right foot forward, holds his sword with his hand rotated with the thumb up. Both men again hold their left hand at their hip or on their back. The guard position used by the man on the left is very similar to the *Porta di Ferro Larga* position used in mid-sixteenth century Italian sources (e.g. the fourth guard of Viggiani, 1575; see also Leoni, 2010). The cut and parry shown in this plate may represent a continuation from plate 2.

Transcription, Translation and Illustrations - Single Sword

4. A high crossing of the swords (5v)

The two fencers are again both standing with their legs apart, each leading with the right foot and holding his left hand at the back. Each holds his sword at, or slightly above, shoulder height, with their hands held in the position denominated as *Tertia* in Italian rapier fencing sources. The swords are crossed on the inside, above shoulder height. This bind could for instance have resulted from a downward diagonal cut from the right by the fencer on the right, being parried by the fencer on the left. Note that this image gives a clear view on the grip used by the fencer on the right, who clearly does not wrap any fingers around the hilt of his sword, and holds his sword in a rather stiff-fisted grip.

Transcription, Translation and Illustrations - Single Sword

5. A low crossing of the blades at the outside follows (6r)

While each fencer stands in a similar position to that shown in the previous plate, they now hold their swords down, and crossed at the outside. This situation may for instance arise when the fencer on the left parries a reverse blow to his front leg given by the fencer on the right. This could occur as a follow on from the previous plate. Alternatively, the fencers could have arrived in this position if the fencer on the left broke the position of the fencer on the right, by binding his blade downwards and to the right, creating an opening. Such a breaking of the position is also seen on folio 4r of Pieter Bailly's "Cort Bewijs" (Bailly, 1602-1608) from the first decade of the 17th century. (Note that my interpretation of the plate in Bailly differs from the interpretation published by Galas and Steenput, 2011.) One interesting aspect of this image is that the sword of the man on the right can be seen to have a well-pronounced diamond cross-section.

6. A left-handed fencer crosses blades with a right-handed man (6v)

The man on the left holds his sword in his left hand, and stands with his right foot in front. His blade is crossed on the outside of his opponent's blade. His opponent stands with the right foot forward, and holds his sword in the right hand in *Tertia*. These positions may have resulted as the right-handed fencer parried a thrust on his outside line performed by the left-handed fencer (note the raised foot of the left-handed fencer). In contrast to the fencers on the previous illustrations, the free hands are not held at the hip or the back, but rather the arm is thrown back, and the hand is held spread at shoulder or head height (reminiscent of a modern fencing stance). This may have been intended to profile the body.

7. Two fencers in different guard positions (7r)

The man on the left stands upright, with his left foot in front, holding his sword in the right hand in front of his right hip, with his hand held in *Tertia*. His sword points forward and up (the tip is at navel height). He holds his left hand open in front of him, at head height. The man on the right stands with his right foot forward, leaning his torso backwards. He holds his sword at shoulder height or slightly above, with the blade horizontal and pointing forward. Note that his hand is not held rotated in Prima, as might be expected. Instead, his hand is held elevated in a very high *Tertia*. He holds his left hand in front of his body at navel height. Very similar guard positions can for instance be found in the treatises written by Henry de Sainct Didier (1573 – see also Hyatt and Wilson, 2009) and Giacomo di Grassi (Di Grassi, 1570). It is interesting to note that both men hold their left hand near the point of the opposing blade. The same approach appears in the rapier and dagger plates later in this manuscript.

8. Another high bind (7v)

The man on the right stands with the right foot forward, leaning his torso back, and holding his sword up high, pointing forward and down. In contrast to the previous image, he has his thumb downwards with his hand held in an Italian *Prima*. The man on the left also stands right foot forward and is similarly leaning his torso back. He holds his sword high, with the point forward and somewhat down, his hand rotated in *Quarta* or even further, and has bound his opponent's sword from underneath. Having come past the point (which is to the outside of his wrist), he now threatens to thrust his opponent in the opening created. Both men again hold their left hand on their back. The fencing situation shown in this illustration could have followed from the previous plate, with the fencer on the left having come forward with a passing step with the right foot, binding the opponent's sword by rotating his blade upwards. This position is similar to the counter to the *Imbrocade* shown by Thibault (1630 – see Tabula. VIII. Circulus N°. 2.).

9. and 10. An unarmed man using a rather shrewd trick to defend himself against an assailant armed with a sword (8r and 8v)

The first plate shows the assailant, coming forward with his left foot in front, his sword held drawn back horizontally at the hip. His left hand is held forwards, palm upward in a gesture suggesting this might be a mugging. The intended victim, standing still opposite his attacker, appears to remain calm, and while distracting the attacker, brings his left hand up to the rim of his hat. In doing this, he has his thumb rotated to the outside to allow him to directly throw his hat from his head into the opponent's face in one quick motion.

On the next plate, we can see how the would-be victim has made his throw, and used the distraction to rush in, grabbing the wrist of the attacker's sword hand, and turning the situation into a grapple.

A similar distraction can also be seen in Hans Talhoffer's 1459 manuscript "Alte Armatur und Ringkunst" (p. 157), where a man throws his hat in the face of an attacker armed with a spear, in order to distract him from the dagger he throws into his chest.

Rapier and Dagger Fencing

The second section consists of five plates showing sword and dagger fencing. The swords used in this section are similar to the longer, narrower swords shown in the second part of the single sword section, having relatively long, thin blades, and complex hilts with a straight cross, and side rings, but without knuckle bows. The daggers used here have 30-40cm long blades, and crosses that are sharply curved up towards the blade.

1. Two man preparing to fence with sword and dagger (9r)

The fencer on the right is standing with his feet apart, right foot in front, his torso leaning back, and has just drawn his sword and his dagger. The fencer on the left is standing with the right foot forward, and has placed his hands on the hilts of his weapons, preparing to draw them. Note that this illustration is nearly identical in content to the first illustration in the single sword section.

2. A bind with the dagger against the sword (9v)

Both fencers stand in position, with their torsos leaning back. The man on the right is leading with the right foot, holding his sword pointing forward at shoulder height, with his hand held in an Italian *Tertia*. He holds his dagger close to him in front of his hip, pointing forward and somewhat up. The man on the left leads with his left foot, and holds his sword horizontally in front of his hip. He uses his dagger to bind down onto the opponent's sword from the inside, thus creating space for an attack. This situation may have followed upon the previous plate, with the man on the left drawing his weapons and stepping forward to bind the sword of the man on the right who, in the meantime, had lowered his sword into a more threatening position.

Note in that in this plate, both fencers hold their dagger near the point of the opponent's sword. Such positioning of the dagger (high when the opponent's sword is high, low when the opponent's sword is low, and near or against the point of the sword if possible) is seen throughout the rapier and dagger section. Similar placement of the offhand is also seen in the single sword plates (e.g. plate 7 on page 7r).

3. A double bind (10r)

Both fencers stand with the right foot in front, binding their opponent's sword with their dagger. The man on the left binds his opponent's sword on the opponent's outside, with his dagger held pointing up in front of his body, his arm bent. He holds his sword pointing forward at his hip, with his hand held in *Tertia*. The fencer on the right binds down onto his opponent's sword on the opponent's outside, with his dagger held in front of him. He holds his sword at shoulder height, with the thumb down or to the outside (i.e. in an Italian *Secunda* or *Prima*). He stands with his right foot in front, and is leaning his torso back.

It is possible that this illustration represents a continuation from the previous plate. The transition into this position could then have occurred in a number of different ways. For example, the fencer on the right may have changed into *Prima* to disengage over the dagger of his opponent and thrust. The fencer on the left would then have parried this attack to his right using his dagger, passing forward and thrusting between his opponent's weapons with his sword. This attack is in turn parried by the fencer on the right, using his dagger.

This possible sequence may explain why the rather strange looking high *Tertia* position is used, as it allows a very easy disengage over an opponent's dagger parry or bind by transitioning into *Prima*, followed by a thrust between the weapons. Note that thrusts between the weapons are commonly advised in period rapier and dagger treatises, such as for instance Fabris (1606 – see also Leoni, 2005)

4. Two guard positions (10v)

The fencer on the left is standing in a rather deep position, with the left foot in front, and the right knee bent down towards the ground. He has his sword arm hanging down, holding his sword horizontally forward at hip height. He has his left arm stretched forward, with the dagger held slightly above shoulder height, pointing forward and up. Potentially, he arrived in this position after making a passing step back from his position in the previous image, in order to escape from the bind there. The man on the right holds his dagger in front of his body, and his sword above shoulder height, pointing forward, his hand rotated in *Prima*. His position is very similar to the position of the man on the right in the previous plate, except that the man here stands with his left foot in front.

The fencers may have arrived in this position from the position shown in the previous plate, if the fencer on the left stepped back to withdraw in to safety after making his attack. In stepping back, he drew back his blade to disengage this, but kept his dagger extended to cover the line. The fencer on the right may have stepped forward, following his opponent, explaining his change in footing. Note again that the fencer on the left holds his dagger extended high, near the point of the high sword of his opponent. The fencer on the right keeps his dagger low to cover the low line, on which the fencer on the left holds his sword.

5. Another double bind (11r)

The double bind shown here is very similar to the situation shown in the third illustration – both fencers even wear the same clothes. Again, both fencers stand with their right foot in front. This plate likely shows an alternative continuation from plate 2, where the fencer on the right disengages beneath, rather than over, the dagger of his opponent, while keeping his hand in *Tertia*. He then attacks with a thrust between the weapons, but his opponent parries this attack to his right with his dagger, while passing forwards and making his own thrust between the weapons of the fencer on the right. Note that in this attack, the fencer on the left holds the hilt of his sword lifter higher.

Fencing with Dussack and Shield

The next two plates show men dressed in stereotypical Turkish garb, with robes reaching down to below their knees, and turbans, sporting curved blades and oddly-shaped shields with Islamic designs painted on them. Though their appearance in a western European fencing treatise may be surprising, an explanation may be found in the history of the Netherlands. During the early years of the Dutch revolt against Spain (already in 1566), the Dutch leader, William I of Orange, asked the Ottoman Empire for assistance against Catholic Spain. The Ottoman sultan responded with a letter promising military support to the "Lutherans in Flanders and other Spanish provinces, at a time determined by them". Furthermore, trade between the Dutch and the Ottomans existed at least as early as the 1560's[13].

---

13 See Bulut (2001), p112-113. Further indications of Ottoman-Dutch contacts during the early stages of the Dutch revolt are the slogan of the so-called *geuzen* (Dutch rebel troops) "*Liever Turks dan Paaps*" (rather a Turk than a Papist) and the red banners with crescent displayed on their ships.

1. Two man preparing to fence with dussack and shield (11v)

In the first plate, a similar situation is shown as on the first single sword plate and the first sword and dagger plate. The man on the left stands ready to draw his blade, while the man on the right has already done so. He stands with the right foot forward, holding his shield diagonally out in front of his body, and holding his sword up at face height, with his right arm bent, and with the point of the sword aimed back behind his head.

2. Two guard positions with dussack and shield (12r)

In the second plate, both fencers have drawn their blades. The man on the left stands with his left foot in front, holding his left arm outstretched with his shield in front of him. He holds his blade behind his head, ready to strike a diagonal blow from the right. In this position, the straps by which he holds his shield are clearly visible. His opponent stands with the right foot forward, leaning his torso back significantly. He holds his shield in front facing sideways, and holds his sword in a hanging guard above his head, with the point forwards and down, and with his hand held in Prima. This is the correct position to parry a diagonal blow from the right as described by the text.

Rapier and Buckler Fencing

The following three plates in the manuscript show fencers with swords and bucklers. As in most of the manuscript, these swords have narrow, long blades, straight crosses, side rings, and no knuckle bows. The bucklers are about 30cm in diameter. They have rather deep bowls and some of them have edges that slope backwards. Four of the six bucklers shown appear to have an animalistic face painted on the bowl.

1. Two guard positions (12v)

The fencer on the left stands with the left foot forward, holding his buckler with the left hand at chest height, his almost fully stretched arm held out straight in front of him. He holds his sword in front of his hips, pointing down and to the right. A very similar guard position can be found in mid-sixteenth century Italian sources, such as Manciolino (1531) and Marozzo (1536), where it is known as "Coda Lunga e Larga" (see Leoni, 2010). The fencer on the right stands with the right foot in front, and holds his buckler in front of him at, or just below, chest height, and his sword above and somewhat in front of his right shoulder, pointing back over this shoulder. This position is comparable to the "Guardia Alta" in Italian swordplay of the mid-sixteenth century sources, though with the buckler held slightly less extended and somewhat lower than shown there (Leoni, 2010).

2. Two additional guard positions (13r)

The man on the left stands with his left foot in front, his buckler held in front of his shoulder with the arm now fully extended, and he holds his sword held near-horizontal with his right hand just behind his hip. The position shown is similar to the position known as "Coda Lunga e Alta" (as shown in Marozzo (1536) – see Leoni, 2010), though with the sword held more withdrawn, and the point aimed lower. The man on the right stands with the right foot in front, his torso leaning back, the buckler held in front of his body, and his sword held in front of and above the shoulder, pointing forward, hand rotated in Prima. This guard is comparable to the Italian mid-sixteenth century "Guardia di Alicorno", though with the buckler held lower and closer to the body (Leoni, 2010).

3. A low bind (13v)

The third plate shows a low bind. Both men stand with their right foot in front, leaning the torso back, their bucklers held forward at shoulder height, and their swords held at hip height, pointing forward and down. This situation may follow on the previous plate, when the fencer on the left steps back with his left foot, to evade a low reverse strike from the fencer on the right, and parries this strike with his sword, thus illustrating the text on folio 2r ("and if it should happen that your opponent wants to strike you a blow with his rapier below to your legs, you must also parry that with your rapier, and always hold your buckler up high"). Alternatively, the fencer on the left may have stepped forward with his right foot to thrust at the fencer on the right, who reacted by striking down onto the sword of his opponent, parrying this thrust.

Halberd Fencing

Next, five illustrations follow that show men fencing with halberds. The halberds shown are relatively long (~2.5-3m), with a thin long point, and an ornamental-looking blade with a short hook or beak on the back. The blades themselves are crescent-shaped, with additional points protruding at various locations, parallel to the halberd shaft. In all illustrations, the halberds are held in the same grip, with the thumbs underneath the shaft and pointing towards each other (i.e. with the back of each hand facing up). Furthermore, the halberds are held near the end of the shaft, with the hands far apart. Either hand can be the leading hand, and there does not appear to be a correlation between the leading hand and the leading foot. In the first three drawings, the fencers wear the more voluminous type of pantaloons, drooping below the knee, while in the last two illustrations the less spacious type of pantaloons are worn.

1. Two guard positions or a bind (14r)

Both fighters stand with their halberds held nearly horizontal in front of their chins. The halberds are aimed forward, with the blade pointing up. The man on the left leads with his left hand and foot, the man on the right with his right hand and left foot; his left foot is rotated slightly outwards. While this image may just represent two different guard positions, a bind does seem to exist between the two weapons, as could for instance result from a parried thrust.

2. A low bind (14v)

The fighter on the left has stepped forward (still leading with the left foot), binding his opponent's halberd down and around to his outside, i.e. to his own left. In order to achieve the bind shown here, he must have lifted the head of his halberd over the halberd of his opponent and then made a clockwise rotation. The point of his halberd is aimed at the left, leading leg of the other fighter, who is still standing with his left foot in front, holding his halberd on his left side, and with the right hand leading. (Note that in this image the halberd of the man on the left appears significantly shorter than in the other images.)

3. A leg hook (15r)

The fighter on the left moves forward to catch the right ankle of his opponent with the hook of his halberd in order to trip him. In doing so, he appears to have stepped with his right foot forward. This allows him to step back with his right foot to generate the power required to pull the opponent's leg, though he is already pulling it off the ground in his current position. The man on the right again stands with his halberd held horizontal in front of his shoulders, with the right hand in front. He may have just made a passing step back from his position in the previous plate, releasing his halberd from the bind at the same time, and giving away a tempo for the leg hook.

4. Finishing a downed opponent (15v)

Here, the fighter on the left has successfully tripped his opponent, and now points his halberd at his fallen opponent's chest. The fallen fighter may be trying to parry the coming thrust with the shaft of his halberd.

5. A neck hook (16r)

The fencer on the right, who is leading with his left hand and foot, has caught his opponent's neck using the hook of his halberd. The fencer on the left is also leading with the left hand and foot, holding his halberd pointed diagonally forward and down. This illustration may show a counter to the leg hook shown on folio 15r, in which case the fencer on the right would have stepped back with his right foot, swinging his halberd overhead while changing the leading hand. Interestingly, the fencers wear the same clothing as on the previous plate.

Fencing with Pikes

The final three pages show men fencing with long pikes. Despite the title, the fencers use long staffs, roughly six meters long, without sharpened tips. Due to the size of the weapons, the illustrations are spread over two opposing pages, meaning we only have one full illustration, plus one half of a drawing. The first two pages also contain the text regarding fencing with the pike. Interestingly, the pike fencers all wear the more voluminous variation of pantaloons.

Folios 16v & 17r

Transcription:

Dit ist spel inder heeler Spice -- 1595

Inder spicen Spel Behoordij u te voegen wel om uwen Campion te brenghen tonder.

met eenen lustelijk steck van boven naer uwen campion te steken Ende dan terstont zoo moitdie ghy u voughen In u posture met

u hant omhooghe om zynen steck te brenghen tonder ende dan zoo moetdie ghy lichtelijk u voughen

om hem eenen steck te presenteren ende hy nu gereeder waer om u eenen

steck te brenghen zoo moitdy ghy metter syden omvringhen om

synen steck tonder te brenghen.

Translation:

This is the play with the full pike -- 1595

In the play of the pike you have to position yourself well to bring your opponent down, thrusting at your opponent with a hearty thrust from above[14]. And then you must immediately put yourself into your posture with your hand up high to bring down his thrust; and then you must nimbly move yourself to present him a thrust. And if he were more ready to bring you a thrust, then you must twist around with the side[15] to bring down his thrust.

---

14 Here bringing the opponent down should be interpreted as defeating him, though it could more literally mean bringing him to the ground. Alternatively, "...uwen Campion te brenghen tonder. met eenen lustelijk steck van boven naer uwen campion te steken..." could be translated as "...bring your opponent below, to thrust at your opponent with a hearty thrust from above...", i.e. binding down on his pike to create an opening for a thrust on the high line.

15 The segment "zoo moitdy ghy metter syden omvringhen" (then you must twist around with the side) is difficult to translate. We interpret this to indicate that you twist your body around in order to parry the incoming thrust. Alternatively, this segment could indicate that you circle around with the side of your weapon in order to parry, but in this case, the linguistic composition would be strange.

1. Two fencers with pikes in guard positions (16v-17r)

In the first illustration, the fencer on the left stands with his left foot in front, holding his pike horizontally in front of him at chin height. He loosely holds his pike near the butt end with both hands with his hands about one meter apart, and the left hand in front. The backs of the hands are upward, and the thumbs are below the pike.

His opponent similarly holds his pike loosely in both hands, also holding it horizontally but at mouth height. In contrast, the opponent holds the pike on his left side, leading with the right hand, and standing with the left foot in front. His left foot is placed pointing outwards.

Transcription, Translation and Illustrations - Pikes

2. One fencer with pike (17v)

On the second (incomplete) illustration, a man can be seen standing with the left foot in front, and holding his pike horizontally in front of him as on the first page, though slightly higher. His opponent's pike is pointing downward into the floor. One possible explanation is that he has just struck down his opponents thrust and has now raised his pike to threaten his opponent, as is described in the text.

Bibliography

Bailly, Pieter (1602-1608) Cort Bewijs van t'Rapier alleen. 72 F 37, held in: De Koninklijke Bibliotheek, The Hague, Netherlands.

Bulut, Mehmet (2001) Ottoman-Dutch economic relations in the early modern period 1571-1699, Uitgeverij Verloren, Hilversum.

Di Grassi, Giacomo (1570) Ragione di adoprar sicuramente l'arme si da offesa, come da difesa, Giordano Ziletti, & compagni, Venice, Italy.

Fabris, Salvator (1606) De lo Schermo, overo Scienza d'Arme, Henrico Waltkirck, Copenhagen.

Giganti, Nicoletto (1619) Escrime Nouvelle ou Theatre, auquel sont representees diverses manieres de parer et de fraper d'Espee seule, et d'Espee et poignard, Jacques de Zeter, Frankfurt, Germany.

Galas, Matt, and Eli Steenput (2011) The Cort Bewijs of Pieter Bailly – A Dutch rapier manual, circa 1602 – 1608, in: Cognot, Fabris (ed.), Arts de Combat – Théorie & pratique en Europe – XIVe – XXe siècle, Association pour l'Edition et la Diffusion des Etudes Historiques, Paris, France, pp 65-76.

Greer, John Michael (2006) Academy of the Sword – The Mystery of the Spanish Circle in Swordsmanship and Esoteric Arts, Chivalry Bookshelf, Highland Village, Texas.

Hyatt, Robert Preston and Devin Wilson (2009) The single sword of Henry de Sainct-Didier (Traicté contenant les secrets du premier livre sur l'Espée seule), Paladin Press, Boulder, Colorado.

Leoni, Tomasso (2005) Art of dueling, Salvator Fabris' rapier fencing treatise of 1606, Chivalry Bookshelf, Highland Village, Texas.

Leoni, Tomasso (2010) The complete Renaissance swordsman, A guide to the use of all manner of weapons, Antonio Manciolino's Opera Nova (1531), Freelance Academy Press, Wheaton, Illinois.

Manciolino, Antonio (1531) Di Antonio Manciolino Bolognese Opera Nova.

Marozzo, Achille (1536) Opera Nova de Achille Marozzo Bolognese.

de Sainct Didier, Henry (1573) Traicte contenant les Secrets du premier Livre sur l'Espée seule, Jean Mettayer & Matthurin Challenge, Paris, France.

Talhoffer, Hans (1459) Alte Armatur und Ringkunst, Thott 290 2°, held in: Det Kongelige Bibliotek, Kopenhagen, Denmark.

Thibault, Girard (1630) Academie de l'Espée de Girard Thibault d'Anvers, Elsevier, Leiden, Netherlands.

Viggiani, Angelo (1575) Lo Schermo d'Angelo Viggiani dal Montone da Bologna, Giorgio Angelieri, Venice, Italy.